NTS

g Guide

text by Bob Hopkins

JARROLD COLOUR PUBLICATIONS · NORWICH

What is an Annual?

Quite simply a plant that completes its life cycle in one year. That is, having first germinated from a seed itself, it makes all its vegetative growth (stems and leaves), forms flowers, produces its own seeds and then dies naturally within the space of one growing season. The Hardy Annuals typify this cycle exactly. As they withstand late spring frosts, we sow them directly into the open ground where they are to flower.

Many Annuals are not frost hardy but nevertheless are valuable flowers for our summer gardens. We call these Half-hardy Annuals and they are included in the group known as Bedding Plants. Asters, Marigolds and Zinnias are good examples of Half-hardy Annuals. They require the protection of a greenhouse until risk of spring frost has passed, when they can then be safely planted out into their flowering quarters.

Many Half-hardy Bedding Plants are not strictly speaking Annuals at all but Tender, or short-lived, Perennials. As they flower quickly from seed and bloom profusely through the summer months they are very valuable and important in our gardens. Ageratum, Begonias, Geraniums, Impatiens and Petunias are examples of this type. Being Perennials, it is possible to take cuttings or lift plants for over-wintering in frost-free conditions, but it is usually better to start new plants from fresh seed each year.

Why are they good garden plants?

Firstly, because they grow so fast and flower so quickly from seed. Most householders in Britain plant Bedding Plants around their homes during May. These may be young plants grown from seed sown as late as April and most will be showing colour by mid–late June. Secondly, because of their profusion of flower, carried in many cases throughout the summer months until they are cut down by autumn frosts.

They are at their best at the time when the majority of people, even the reluctant gardeners among us, most enjoy and appreciate our gardens – the summer months. Thirdly, the wide choice of plants for all situations – sun or shade, moist or dry, sheltered or exposed aspects, even north-facing open beds, or containers such as tubs, windowboxes, suspended baskets, etc. – ensures that you can beautify any part of your home environment in the way you like best.

Which brings me to point four – the opportunities for *change* that Annuals give us. We all like to experiment and make changes in our environment, and in our gardens Annuals enable us to make changes more quickly and at lower cost than any other type of plant. The wide diversity of plant types and flower colours available can be likened to the colour cards and material swatches of interior decorators and they enable us to be as adventurous. More so in reality because with Annuals as the 'paint and wallpaper' of our exterior decorating we can change the colours and mood each year.

What are their likes and dislikes?

All Annuals and Bedding Plants are easily grown in any reasonable garden soil – some will flourish even in poor soils. The majority are sun-lovers – certainly the Hardy Annuals – but there are good shade-tolerant plants among Bedding Plants that brighten those difficult corners where no other flower seems willing to bloom. (Impatiens and Begonias are good examples.) All Annuals need adequate moisture in their early stages of growth, which the gardener must apply if nature won't. At maturity, bright sunny weather encourages maximum flower production, and shelter from strong, gusting winds can be important, especially for taller cultivars.

Summer bedding plants at their best.

How are they best used in gardens?

(a) Bedding Plants

There can be very few gardeners who do not use Annuals, particularly Half-hardy Bedding Plants, and in many instances they form the major part of their summer displays. Our summer gardens would be very different places without them, but it is true that many plantings would benefit if more imaginative thought went into their planning. For maximum effect separate colours should be used more widely in harmonising or contrasting combinations. Go into any of the better public parks in the summer and notice how the dramatic effects they achieve are due to the careful association of specific colours. Mixtures planted as such are used much less frequently.

Don't overlook the value of contrasting forms and heights as well as colours. Many bedding Annuals are so compact and uniform in all their characteristics that on their own, or with others of similar height, they can appear monotonous to the eye, despite brilliant colouring. A few plants placed among them of another variety or type that is taller and of a different structure (i.e. branching, open or erect growth) will enhance the whole and retain the interest of the onlooker. The same is true of flower forms, where the tall thrusting spikes of Antirrhinums, Pentstemons or Salvias add importance to Begonias, Petunias, Marigolds, etc.

Some people maintain that Bedding Plants are too bothersome and costly and therefore never buy them, filling their gardens with roses or shrubs instead. While understanding their reasoning, I feel that their conclusion is wrong. Why? Because, having filled most of the garden with a permanent planting, they have provided for themselves an ideal situation in which they can enjoy the summer brilliance that only Annuals can give. A mere dozen or so, carefully chosen and placed, will liven up a shrub border. The bare ground beneath the long withered shanks of a favourite, but ageing, rosebush will sustain Ageratum, Begonias, Impatiens, Lobelias or Pansies to the advantage of both. The varied contours and textures provided by the background foliage of shrubs give a restful effect that carries the brightest coloured Annuals without any appearance of garish vulgarity.

(b) Hardy Annuals

Entire borders used to be grown using numerous varieties of these cheap, simple flowers but this is less usual now. Instead they are valued and commonly used as fillers for spaces in Perennial and shrub borders, and many gardeners leave space specially for them in smaller beds. They are seeded directly into the border soil where they are to flower. Some can be sown in late summer to flower the following year, but the most favoured time to sow is April, as soon as the soil has become friable and can be levelled and firmed. The seed may be broadcast thinly and evenly and then raked in or, better, sown in shallow drills. It is easier to distinguish seedlings when they first emerge in drills, and subsequent thinning and weeding is simplified. Spray lightly with water after sowing and if the soil dries repeat until germination is complete.

Are there any special rules for planting Bedding Plants?

Weeds

Like all other plants you grow, clean weed-free soil will save a lot of work. If your soil contains a lot of quick-germinating annual weed seeds, do not sow Annual flowers direct but set out young plants. This will give them a head start over the weeds.

Soil texture

Soil that contains plenty of organic matter, i.e. peat, compost, etc., will have the necessary loose, spongy structure that retains moisture, promotes quick rooting and will not bake hard and crack in dry spells.

Fertiliser

A light dressing of a general purpose fertiliser may be scattered and worked in before planting. Avoid those with high nitrogen levels which may produce too much leaf and stem at the expense of flowers. Plants growing in containers will need extra applications through the summer on account of their restricted root run.

Begonia *'Scarletta' and* Alyssum *'Snowdrift', with 'dot' plants for added interest.*

Planting

Choose vigorous sturdy young plants from your supplier. Don't hesitate to take his advice if in doubt, especially if you are uncertain of the correct time to plant in your locality. Soak the plants *thoroughly*, at least half an hour before planting, or overnight. Don't plant too deeply, but make sure the rootball is covered by 1·5 cm of soil to prevent undue drying out, and to help anchor the plant securely.

Spacing

Don't overcrowd them. Adequate space, light and air makes sturdy plants that remain healthy and pest free. 20 cm is about right for smaller compact types such as Begonias, Alyssum, etc.; 30–38 cm for the vigorous ones.

Note: Most Bedding Plants will spread over a much greater space than they are usually allowed – F1 hybrid Petunia plants can grow 60–75 cm across in isolation.

Watering, Maintenance and Aftercare

After planting out, water each plant in thoroughly, giving half a cupful to the soil at the base of each stem – a casual overhead sprinkle from a rosecan is *not* adequate. There is little else to do apart from soak-watering in dry spells and hoeing any weeds between plants in the early stages. A good Bedding Plant is trouble-free and most flower continuously. Only the old flower or seed heads will need removing.

Raising your own Half-hardy Bedding Plants from seed

1 Buy the best varieties you can afford – F1 hybrids generally give more colour and flowers, are often easier to grow, and are no more work to plant out and look after than cheap inferior types. Follow instructions on packet.

2 Sow seed thinly on moistened peat/sand compost. Cover seeds with thin layer of compost or vermiculite. Very fine seeds such as Begonia should not be covered.

3 Wrap tray closely in clear polythene film and place in warm situation (65–70 °F if at all possible). A heated greenhouse or a windowsill in a warm room will serve but protect tray from direct rays of sun. Inspect daily for signs of germination. Tap the covering to clear condensation so that you can see any seedlings through the film. (Do not unwrap.)

4 When seeds have all germinated, ventilate film cover gradually over 2–3 days by loosening the wrapping from ends and sides.

5 When large enough to handle, transplant seedlings into trays or small pots, using a potting compost. A tray with thin-walled unit pots will provide all the advantages of pot culture with the simple handling of a tray. Units of 24 and 40 are most suitable.

6 Water in and grow on carefully with plenty of light and air. When the plants are large enough, move them to a cold frame for hardening off prior to planting out.

7 Regular attention is vital to success – visit your seedlings and inspect them **every day**, preferably morning and evening. If you are unable – or unwilling – to give them this small amount of your time daily, buy your plants instead.

Bedding Plants for Special Purposes

A Edging Beds and Borders As alternatives to Alyssum and Lobelia try Ageratum, *Antirrhinum* 'Floral Carpet' and 'Pixie', Dwarf Begonias, *Cineraria* 'Silver Dust', *Dianthus* 'Magic Charms', French Marigold 'Pascal', *Phlox drummondii* and Tagetes.

B Hot, Sun-scorched Situations The majority of Annuals love the sun, but these will withstand more than most others: Carnations and Dianthus, Gazanias, Geraniums, American and French Marigolds, Mesembryanthemum, Nasturtiums, Petunias, Phlox and Verbenas. Plant a little closer than usual and water well in the early stages. Once established they can survive for quite long periods with minimal moisture.

C Patios and Paved Terraces These areas both absorb and reflect the heat of the sun, and temperatures on and around them can climb very high in midsummer. All Annuals will do well here if frequently watered, but if water is not freely available choose plants from Group B, and also Zinnias.

D Shady and North-facing Areas The first choice, especially if shade is dense, has to be that Queen of the Shade, Impatiens or Busy Lizzie. Both Tuberous- and Fibrous-rooted Begonias are excellent, and *Calceolaria* 'Sunshine', Lobelias, Pansies and Ageratum will all serve here. As all plants grow taller than average in shade, choose only varieties of low or medium height.

E Annual Hedges Robust branching Annuals that need little or no support will quickly grow into beautiful low, flowering hedges. *Lavatera* 'Silver Cup' and 'Mont Blanc', Jubilee African Marigolds and Sweet Pea 'Jet-Set' all give weeks of flower.

F Hanging Baskets, Windowboxes and Tubs Choose Annuals that have a low or spreading habit so that their branches will cascade over the edges of the container. Petunias are among the finest, giving an avalanche of colour. Impatiens and Begonias do well in sheltered situations. Calceolaria, Nasturtiums, Phlox and Verbena adapt well. With several plants crowded into a restricted area regular attention is needed, particularly daily watering. Give extra fertiliser when the plants are fully flowering.

Some of the better Bedding Plants

In a book such as this it is neither possible nor appropriate to list all the many varieties of Hardy and Half-hardy Annuals that could be grown in British gardens. I have therefore restricted my choice to those varieties that I consider to be of greatest value at the present time. Generally I have been able to reduce considerably the number of items by listing mixtures rather than a host of separate colours of the same strain; my commendation of the mixture applies equally to the separate colours.

A good proportion of my recommendations are recent introductions and are good examples of the improvements being made each year by modern plant breeders. I am certain that all will give satisfaction; some may generate increased enthusiasm; a few, perhaps, a feeling of excitement for this cheerfully brilliant and indispensable group of garden plants.

**These items may also be sown directly into the open ground during late May and early June where the plants are to flower.*

Ageratum

Beautiful long-lasting subjects, superb whether massed or used as edging plants. Fluffy flowerheads cover the plants and are produced over a long period. Ageratums also make long lasting houseplants in a light window. All varieties are frost-tender.

'Blue Angel' (F1 hybrid) A mid-blue variety, uniform and compact, with a very long flowering season. A good, all-purpose variety. 12 cm.

'Blue Blazer' (F1 hybrid) The first hybrid Ageratum and the most widely grown. Very early flowering mid-blue which can sometimes 'burn' out in hot dry summers. Good uniformity and makes a fine pot plant. 12 cm.

'Blue Danube' (F1 hybrid) The finest variety yet introduced, uniform, low spreading habit, plus incredible stamina; its re-flowering capabilities keep it smothered in colour from first flowers until autumn frost. A light blue, the best there is. 15 cm.

'Blue Mink' Very large flowerheads, robust upright plants of rather variable uniformity. A very reliable variety whose vigour ensures a good performance in most seasons. Flowerheads of mid blue. 20–25 cm.

There is also a white variety **'Spindrift'** which is very early flowering but which tends to 'burn' out in hot seasons.

Alyssum

Although listed in the Hardy Annuals section, Alyssum is, of course, used in huge numbers as a transplanted bedding plant. See Hardy Annuals list for varieties.

Antirrhinum

One of the great standbys of the old traditional English summer gardens, Snapdragons remain one of the best adapted plants for our cool average summer. They flourish in open sunny situations, yet, being tolerant of low temperatures, can be planted out early, in late March or April, if conditions permit. A very wide range of colours and forms is available in heights that vary from the dwarfest at 10 cm to tall border giants of 130 cm. Most varieties are improved by pinching out the tops of the plants to encourage a bushy, base-branching habit, once they are established in their flowering positions, and all benefit by removal of the old seed pods after flowering. F1 hybrid varieties are strongly recommended for the finest possible displays.

'Little Darling' has open-throated flowers.

◀ Snapdragons are always colourful and reliable.

SNAPDRAGON FLOWERED.

Coronette Hybrids (F1 hybrid) Acknowledged world-wide as the finest bedding Snapdragons ever raised, the Coronette strain is distinguished by numerous robust heavy flower spikes of unmatched uniformity and by its sturdy stems and very vigorous rooting rendering it almost immune to windblow. A bed of Coronette in flower is a sight to be remembered. If you want to grow the best, this is the one. 40 cm.

'Monarch' Mixture (Rust resistant) A strain of the traditional English Snapdragons that has been specially bred for resistance to the rust diseases which attack Antirrhinum foliage in midsummer and curtail the flowering season in some districts. A very wide range of colours. 35 cm.

'Floral Carpet' (F1 hybrid) A superb extra dwarf, bush flowered Snapdragon, very early flowering and ideal for rockeries and even edging. Very uniform and free-flowering with good recovery and repeat flowering. 20 cm.

'Rocket Hybrids' (F1 hybrids) The tallest (130 cm) of the 'Snaps' and suitable only for borders where they can be given some support. Magnificent spikes on long stems that are superb for cutting. Rather late to flower and not suitable for massed bedding.

TRUMPET-FLOWERED

Modern plant breeders have produced new forms of Antirrhinums that are unrecognisable as Snapdragons, the flowers being of tubular form with open, trumpet-shaped throats like a Pentstemon or Freesia. They are very colourful indeed. Coupled with this novel flower form is very early flowering plus an ability to produce further flushes of bloom that is not found in 'Snapdragon' types. All are unique and valuable new Bedding Plants that will liven up any garden. Really worth growing.

'Bright Butterflies' (F1 hybrid) The tallest (75 cm) in this class. Open-throated single flowers in a range of colours. A very choice variety for the back of the border.

'Little Darling' (F1 hybrid) At 30 cm the perfect bedding version of 'Bright Butterflies'. Compact, bushy growth, early and free-flowering in very bright colours. An outstanding introduction in every way.

'Pixie' Mixed (F1 hybrid) Of low, mounded, bush or carpeting habit of growth, the plants are smothered in 'Butterfly'-type flowers. Pixie is quicker to flower than any other Antirrhinum and its ability to keep on producing blooms gives it the longest flowering season of any cultivar. Very suitable for late sowings in March or even April. 25 cm.

'Madame Butterfly' Mixed (F1 hybrid) Double-petalled florets on long sturdy stems resemble small Azaleas, making a superb cut flower. The plants are base-branching but are rather weak-rooted so need some additional support. Another unique variety for the back of the border. 60–75 cm.

'Sweetheart' Mixed The double Azalea-flowered form of 'Little Darling', and even earlier. A very attractive bedding variety that will repay pinching back in the early stages of growth. The colours are soft and harmonious and are produced over a long period. Flowers early at 20 cm, final height is 30 cm.

Asters*

Their richly coloured flowers are produced in late August and September when many other bedding plants are past their peak, and therefore bring a welcome new warmth to our gardens in late summer. There are many types to choose from: shaggy, quilled, and

Aster *Dwarf 'Queen' Mixed.*

Begonia *'Myzar' has extra large flowers.*

needle- or thread-petalled flowers; fluffy incurving forms that look like greenhouse chrysanthemums; rounded button, powderpuff, and cushion-centred varieties; and the single-flowered forms, useful for cut-flower arrangements. Plant habit ranges from ultra-dwarf for edging and front of low borders to tall, upright, long-stemmed giants for cutting or filling-in among Perennials and shrubs in your borders.

As bedding plants we only need to consider here the bushy and dwarfer varieties that are most generally offered and which are reliable and trouble-free.

DOUBLE-FLOWERED

'Ostrich Plume' Mixed (45 cm) The traditional double-flowered bedding Aster in Britain and most probably the variety you would receive if you were merely to ask for 'double Asters' at your local garden centre or nursery. Large feathery, double flowers have long petals that curl and interlace to give a very attractive appearance. All the colours in Asters are present (except yellow); violet, pink, red, rose, lavender-blue and white. The freely-branched plants have stems long enough for cutting.

Dwarf Bedding Mixed (20 cm) This ultra-dwarf form has increased in popularity very rapidly in recent years and many named mixtures are now offered that are rather similar. All should give complete satisfaction – **'Colour Carpet'**, **'Queen'**, **'Thousand Wonders'**, **'Roundabout'** – and can be planted with confidence.

The plants all grow low and in the form of a mounded dome, giving a very formal appearance. Uniformity of habit, flower-size and colour is exceptional and they are ideal for edging or massing, in any open situation. Although so very dwarf, please do not plant them on a rockery – the large powderpuff-shaped flowers, in typical strong Aster colours on such dwarf plants in this situation only result in a 'plastic' effect!

'Milady' Mixed (25 cm) Beautifully formed incurving flowers give 'Milady' its unique distinction among dwarf Asters. Compact, rather upright habit, excellent weather resistance and freedom of flowering make this a very good subject for tubs.

SINGLE FLOWERED

'Madeleine' Mixed (Super Sinensis) Not really single as the flowers are composed of several rows of broad petals around a golden-yellow eye. Despite their large size, and their height (80 cm), these flowers do not become rain-sodden and weighted down like the full doubles and so they always remain tidy. Long stems are produced very freely, making 'Madeleine' a fine source of cut flowers.

Begonia *'Nonstop' Mixed thrives in most situations.*

Begonia (Fibrous Rooted)

The ever-blooming Dwarf Semperflorens type of Begonia really typifies what a good Bedding Plant ought to be. Early to flower, it is smothered in bright coloured blossoms throughout the summer until autumn frosts. Once it starts flowering it is almost impervious to any sort of weather, rain or shine, in full sun or shade. The only condition that will spoil it is extreme cold – summer hail will cut it to pieces, and the first frost will kill it. Do not plant out until all risk of frost has passed.

The choice of varieties in this group can be bewildering when you study a collection of seed catalogues. However, if you bear in mind that the inherent good qualities of this plant virtually guarantee its garden performance, irrespective of varietal name, you may happily make your choice by sticking in a pin! Reds all tend to look alike, as do the pinks, roses and whites; the same applies to bronze-leaved and green-leaved varieties. When buying plants, take whatever variety catches your eye – most commercially produced Begonia plants are F1 hybrids and completely dependable.

From what I have just written it would obviously be inappropriate for me now to give a long list of varieties that may only confuse. Therefore I mention the few varieties below that are widely acknowledged to be the most popular sellers and which, being bred in Europe, are especially suited to our particular climate. All are F1 hybrids. 15 cm.

DWARF VARIETIES

'Organdy' Mixture The biggest seller worldwide for twenty years and still unbeaten. Contains both bronze-leaved and green-leaved varieties.

'Cocktail' Mixture A mixture of dark-leaved varieties only, from the same breeder as 'Organdy'. Extremely glossy, deep-bronze foliage so bright as to appear lacquered.

'Belle Vista' Mixture Green-leaved varieties only in a very wide range of colours; performs exceptionally well in our average English summer.

'Linda' Bright rose-pink flowers, fresh green foliage and very neat habit of growth.

'Scarletta' Broad, bushy green-leaved plants are covered with bright orange-scarlet flowers all summer.

SPECIAL VARIETIES

Two new types of Semperflorens Begonias for bedding are also worth a place in our gardens. A development from France combines much larger flowers on vigorous yet still compact plants similar to the preceding varieties, and they are proving to be very reliable and weatherproof. Look out for **'Myzar'**, bright scarlet, and **'Venus'**, brilliant rose-pink, two really exciting introductions. 20 cm.

Of taller, more graceful habit are giant-flowered, long-stemmed bronze-leaved **'Danica'** and green-leaved **'Fortuna'**; each of these Danish varieties is available in scarlet or bright rose. 30–40 cm.

Begonia (Tuberous Rooted)

This is another plant that has been transformed by modern plant breeding into one of the most reliable of Bedding Plants yet it still retains the exotic glamorous appeal of the old varieties. They give an unequalled show of colour in both partial shade or full sun. They will not thrive in the rather arid conditions that their fibrous-rooted cousins can tolerate, but, provided the soil is kept moist they are one of the most rewarding plants you can grow. They have the additional attraction of flowering even more brightly in late summer and early autumn since the cool damp air at that time of year provides the humidity in which they revel – they sparkle like jewels when the Petunias, etc. can no longer perform. They lack frost resistance and the first one will finish them off.

'Nonstop' Mixed (F1 hybrid) A really remarkable development that will remain a classic for years. Large 8 cm fully double flowers are produced freely throughout the season from June until the first frost of autumn. Unlike the traditional giant-flowered type grown from dormant tubers, this seed-raised strain is self-branching and compact. Dark-green foliage sets off the flowers to perfection. Colours include apricot, bright red, orange, bright rose, warm pink, salmon and yellow. 30 cm.

Pure yellow Calceolaria *'Sunshine', edged with Marigold 'Honeycomb' and interplanted with* Antirrhinum *'Coronette Crimson'.*

Cineraria *'Silver Dust'.*

Bedding Dahlias are real space fillers.

Calceolaria rugosa

The hardy outdoor relative to the well-known indoor pot plant, Calceolaria rugosa *was rarely seen in private gardens. Its durability to most weather conditions and continuous flowering throughout the summer were much appreciated by parks departments who needed bright pure yellow colouring for their formal schemes. Then only available by slow and uncertain propagation from cuttings, seed-raised varieties have since been introduced that have ensured its much wider distribution and use. It is another plant that adapts readily to either sun or shade and so can be placed in almost any garden situation, provided that the soil is watered occasionally. In well-drained and sheltered situations, it can survive the winter and come up again for several years.*

'Sunshine' (F1 hybrid) The finest variety ever raised and particularly successful in tubs, windowboxes and hanging baskets. Vigorous yet wiry stems support a profusion of pure yellow pouched flowers. Performs very well in our rather cool summers and whether bedded, tubbed, boxed or suspended, 'Sunshine' is superb. 30 cm.

Carnation

Generally too slow to flower and not really profuse enough to be considered a really good bedding plant, Carnations are nevertheless very useful for bringing interest to mixed borders. Being very hardy, they can be planted out quite early but don't expect to see much colour before mid-August. They enjoy great popularity among gardeners because of their attractive scent and their traditional use as cut flowers for weddings, birthdays and similar sentimental occasions.

'Giant Chabaud' Mixed The most generally grown annual Carnation, with sweetly scented, double flowers and a range of colours. At 45–60 cm it needs support.
'Dwarf Bouquet' or **'Baby' Mixed** 25 cm plants that are very compact and thus better for general bedding use as they require no support.
'Knight' Mixed (F1 hybrid) A new American development that combines the compactness of the dwarf type with improved earliness. Flower quality is superb but price is inevitably higher. Likely to be offered only as single pot-grown plants and certainly a breakthrough for the true Carnation enthusiast. 30 cm.

Cineraria maritima

'Silver Leaf' or 'Dusty Miller' is a silver foliage plant that has achieved tremendous popularity in recent years. Very hardy and of easy culture, it provides superb contrast with its lacy, decorative foliage. Very effective as an edging or massed in groups.

'Silver Dust' The finest variety, compact and relatively slow-growing. The finely cut leaves appear almost snowy white and the plants are very uniform. This is also a surprisingly good indoor foliage plant for mixed bowls and planters. 20 cm.

Dahlia

Bedding Dahlias are usually raised from seed every year, although the tubers may be lifted and stored over-winter for planting out the following season. Relatively undemanding, with a long flowering season, they are one of the best space fillers you can grow. Early to bloom if sown mid-February, they flower more and more profusely as the summer passes and will continue well into the autumn if it is mild and frost-free.

'Coltness' Hybrids The most popular single-flowered mixture. Dwarf compact plants carry large rounded flowers of broad overlapping petals in a nice range of bright colours. Really reliable. 50 cm.

'Redskin' A most unusual mixture with dark-bronze foliage. Flowers are large and semi-double and the colours are delightful and unique. A really good variety for flower arrangements. 50 cm.

'Rigoletto' Extra dwarf and compact plants with freely borne double and semi-double flowers in a range of colours. The earliest dwarf double Dahlia to flower. 30 cm.

'Unwins' Dwarf Hybrids Semi-double flowers in a vast colour range on bushy upright plants. Not as early flowering as 'Rigoletto' and more vigorous, but indispensable where a larger plant is required. A world-famous variety. 60 cm.

'Collarette Dandy' An interesting novelty variety, each of the single flowers has a central collar of small petals of a contrasting colour surrounding the eye. Bushy, early and free-flowering. 60 cm.

Dianthus *'Magic Charms' is superb in open sunny situations.*

Dianthus

Very striking bedding plants of easy culture that have been much improved in recent years. The new F1 hybrid varieties have introduced colours and qualities not previously seen in this section. Tolerant of low temperatures, they may be planted out quite early. All varieties mentioned have single flowers.

'Baby Doll' Very large flowers with beautiful rounded petals. Colours are crimson, pink, rose and white and most of the flowers have a contrasting central zone. May be sown directly into border soil outdoors from April. 15 cm.

'Magic Charms' (F1 hybrid) The most eye-catching Dianthus ever raised, the plants really blaze with colour. When in full flower the foliage is virtually invisible, covered by the fringe-petalled florets. The exceptional range of colours includes a scarlet so bright you could almost warm your hands against it and some unique speckled bicolours. Praised by everybody who grows it. 15 cm.

'Snow Fire' (F1 hybrid) A quite sensational variety that performs superbly in any sunny situation. Each flower is white with a large, dramatically contrasting, scarlet centre. Bushy, self-branching habit with stiff stems and attractive silvery-green foliage make this a worthy companion to 'Magic Charms'. 20 cm.

'Queens Court' Mixed (F1 hybrid) A new introduction that is somewhat suggestive of a Sweet William, with an open, informal style. The flowers are carried in profusion over the whole plant; colours are really bright and varied. 35 cm.

Gazania

Exotic members of the Daisy family, the peacocks of the tribe! They must be planted in a warm situation for their wonderful flowers to open fully. Hardy and very easily grown, they will provide pleasure and even excitement until the end of summer. Any of the mixture of ***'Choice Hybrids'*** *offered should give satisfaction. The variety* ***'Sunshine'****, which is by far the largest and most erotic, is rather slower to bloom and should therefore be planted out as early as possible. 30 cm.*

Diverse types of containers can create special focal points.

Geranium

In no other species has there been seen such a total transformation as we have witnessed in this invaluable bedding plant over the past ten years. Seed-raised bedding geraniums have been lifted from nowhere to the front rank of popular garden plants by what is probably the most intensive and costly series of modern flower-breeding programmes ever undertaken. The new F1 hybrids have secured for themselves a position of importance equal to the best cutting-propagated varieties.

With superb base-branching compact habit, unrivalled flower production plus sustained vigour for late-summer performance, modern seed-raised Geraniums get better and better as the season goes on. Whether for massed bedding, tubs or patio planting, they are superb.

Of the many now available I recommend the following, single-flowered varieties for all-round excellence. 30–40 cm.

ZONED-LEAF VARIETIES

'Cherie', salmon-pink; **'Grenadier'**, intense salmon-red; **'Mustang'**, a brilliant Crampel scarlet; **'Ringo' series**, red, rose, salmon and scarlet; **'Salmon Express'**, warm bright salmon.

GREEN-LEAF VARIETIES

'Heidi', a beautiful salmon and white bicolour; **'Iceberg'**, purest white; **'Red Express'**, solid rich red; **'Fire Flash'**, sizzling fiery scarlet; and **'Sprinter'** – 'Old Faithful' – the reliable time-tested, salmon-red variety that has adorned the gardens in front of Buckingham Palace since Jubilee Year 1977. For a windowsill or conservatory **'Playboy' Mixed** carries brilliantly coloured single flowers in large heads on extra compact, dwarf plants. The contrasting foliage is a very rich dark green. 25 cm.

Helichrysum*

'Strawflowers', previously known to most people – if at all – only in a beheaded, dried condition as part of small formal decorative ornaments, Helichrysum is now available in a dwarf-growing form that makes it a novel and interesting bedding plant.

'Bright Bikinis' Mixed Very free-flowering mixture of vivid colours. Bushy, self-branching plants requiring little attention can be relied on to maintain bright, cheerful appearance for a long period. Good for cutting and drying, too. 30 cm.

Heliotrope

The rich, heavy fragrance of this fine, old-fashioned plant, 'Cherry Pie', is unique in our gardens. The violet-purple and lavender colours associate particularly well with yellow flowers such as African and French Marigolds. Not all plants are scented and the strongest fragrance is found in plants propagated from cuttings. 50 cm.

Hibiscus

'Giant Mallow' is not a bedding plant at all except in very warm favourable situations but a superb specimen 'fun' plant for an outdoor suntrap or a conservatory.

'Southern Belle' (F1 Hybrid) Enormous single flowers almost a foot across justify the name 'Sun-hat Plant'. Needing lots of space, warmth, water and feeding, they repay your labours with flowers of deep red, rose, pink and white in late summer. 150 cm.

Hibiscus *'Southern Belle' is a real crowd-puller!*

Impatiens

'Busy Lizzie' is a well-known popular pot plant for the house or conservatory; modern strains of Impatiens are now bred for use as outdoor bedding plants. As such, they are now unquestionably one of the finest flowers that can be grown in British gardens, easily outperforming their house – and pot – bound sisters and rivalling almost every other type of bedding plant grown. It is only really unhappy in an arid, sun-scorched situation; everywhere else it flourishes. Nowhere is it more valuable than when brightening those difficult shady spots that are otherwise the despair of so many gardeners. Truly the 'Queen of the Shade'.

Virtually any Impatiens will perform well in shade, whether heavy or filtered, but for superb performance in all situations you can rely on these latest F1 hybrid varieties. Grow them anywhere – in pots, tubs, planters, baskets, strawberry barrels, windowboxes, or massed beds. 20–25 cm.

"**'Futura'**, especially good for hanging baskets; **'Grand Prix'**, the largest-flowered variety; **'Minette'**, the most profuse multiflora strain; **'Novette'**, neat mounds of bold flowers; **'Super Elfin'**, a real ground-hugging habit; and **'Zig-Zag' Mixed** with all colours splashed with contrasting white stars.

Lavatera*

Although listed in the Hardy Annuals section the new dwarf varieties ***'Mont Blanc'*** *and* ***'Silver Cup'*** *are just as reliable transplanted as bedding plants. Ask for them at your Garden Centre.*

Lobelia

With white Alyssum, Lobelias are the most widely used edging plant in summer. Good, too, for bedding in filtered shade situations, especially the variety 'Sapphire'.

DWARF VARIETIES

'Cambridge Blue', soft azure-blue; **'Crystal Palace'**, deep blue, bronze foliage; **'Mrs Clibran'**, dark blue with contrasting white eye.

TRAILING VARIETIES

'Sapphire', the finest variety for baskets, etc.; **'Blue Cascade'**, bright Cambridge blue; **'Red Cascade'**, novel carmine-red.

Impatiens *flower continuously until the first autumn frosts.*

Impatiens *'Novette'.*

Impatiens *'Zig-Zag' Scarlet.*

Lavatera *'Silver Cup'.*

Lobelia *'Cambridge Blue'.*

Marigold, African*

Well known for their large rounded flowers, in shades of orange, gold and yellow. Recent, vastly improved varieties have made African Marigolds one of the most useful summer annuals in Britain. Their robust vigour has always guaranteed success from quite simple culture and this has been maintained in new dwarf forms. The breeders have been so successful in reducing the typical height of the older varieties that the plants of one strain are dwarfer even than many French Marigolds. With massive 10 cm, sponge-like flowers on 15–20 cm plants it has the proportions, grace and charm of Giles' Grandma! (I do not recommend it here!)

'Climax' and **'Gold Coin' Series (F1 hybrids)** Really breathtaking flowers up to 13 cm across on tall, exceptionally strong and vigorous plants. Quite incredible when in full flower. 100 cm.

'Jubilee' Series (F1 hybrids) Probably the most generally useful of the spectacular new hybrids. Exceptionally uniform plants that branch freely and are covered with large fully double flowers. They make a fine flowering low hedge. 60 cm.

'Lady' Series (F1 hybrids) I regard this as the limit of acceptable dwarfness. Very neat, tidy plants have very dark-green foliage to contrast with the freely produced double flowers. 45 cm.

'Crackerjack' Mixed This old mixture still turns in a 'value-for-money' show that cannot be ignored. Less vigour and uniformity than the hybrids, of course. 80–100 cm.

Marigold, French

One of the most extensively planted summer annuals, with an unrivalled record of reliability. Once planted out, they need little attention. Any variety of the many available should give satisfaction and since most are bought as plants in flower, names tend to be unimportant. The list below represents the best of recent introductions.

'Pascal' Low-growing plants with large single golden flowers, each petal blotched maroon. Quite superb. 15 cm.

'Boy' Series Fully double flowers in a bright range of colours. All flowers have a contrasting central crest of orange or gold. The best dwarf double for edging, free-flowering over a very long period. 15 cm.

'Super Crested' Series This type of Marigold is now very widely grown. Flowers are larger and produced earlier than previous strains and the plants stay compact throughout. Separate varieties are **'Goldfinch'**, golden yellow; **'Gold Rush'**, maroon and gold; **'Gold Strike'**, rich gold; **'Honeycomb'**, reddish bronze with golden picotee edge; **'Panther'**, deep crimson; **'Queen Bee'**, red and golden yellow. 25 cm.

African-French Hybrids (F1 hybrids)

The result of crossing the two types is a dwarf bushy plant in the French style, with extra vigour and rather larger double flowers that are produced extremely freely and continuously. They do not look particularly impressive as young plants, but don't be deceived – these Marigolds have performance-plus! Certainly to be preferred to the ultra-dwarf pure African type, they combine the best qualities of each parent and can be planted with confidence.

'Honey Bee', bright yellow; **'Sunrise'**, light orange and red; **'Copper Canyon'**, light coppery bronze; **'Big Shot'**, deep gold; **'Nell Gwyn'**, giant golden-yellow single flowers. 35 cm.

French Marigold 'Gold Rush'. Marigolds are among the most reliable of summer bedding plants.

Marigolds come in all sizes! Foreground 'Golden Boy', centre 'Lady' Series, background 'Jubilee' Mixed.

Mesembryanthemum

'Livingstone Daisy', a distinctive and very well-known summer bedding plant, is one of the few annuals that does not look out of place on a rockery. A wonderful performer in any hot dry sunny position, the glistening petals of its daisy-like flowers open in bright sunlight to form a shimmering iridescent carpet of exotic colours. 8 cm.

Nemesia

Another great British favourite, so well known as almost to need no further description. Always does well under cool conditions, so is particularly useful in northern areas. Very quick to flower, the plants are very soon covered in the most wonderful range of colours imaginable. Under cool conditions will flower for weeks on end and will then throw up another flush of flower if the earlier stems are sheared off just as they start to look 'tatty'. ***'Carnival'****, large flowered with sturdy vigorous habit, is the best mixture to grow. 25 cm.*

Nicotiana

Tall and graceful, evening-flowering white Sweet Tobacco used to be planted in twos and threes to provide fragrance rather than flamboyance. Modern breeding has now produced dwarf, early-flowering varieties that remain open throughout the day, flowering profusely in a fine range of colours. A first-class new bedding plant has been born. Alas, all is not gain, for the scent has almost completely gone.

'Crimson Rock' (F1 hybrid) The first of the bush-flowering hybrids and still as good as any. Bright warm carmine-crimson flowers stay open all day. 60 cm.
'Nicki' Mixed (F1 hybrid) An outstanding day-blooming mixture, free-flowering and very uniform. Red, rose, pink, lime and white colours. 45 cm.
'Evening Fragrance' A tall-growing, old-style plant that opens its flowers only in the evening but has exceptional fragrance for a mixture of colours. 90 cm.

Mesembryanthemums really sparkle in the sun.

Nicotiana *'Nicki' Mixed.*

◀ Nemesia *'Carnival' Mixed.*

F1 Hybrid Pansies.

Baskets relieve flat surfaces.

Pansies

Not usually considered as an important summer bedding plant since they tend to 'go off' in summer heat. However, they are very valuable in moist soil in light, filtered shade situations and also north and east facing beds where a tall hedge or building screens them from fierce afternoon sun. Choose F1 hybrid varieties for their extra vigour.

Pentstemon

Their stately weather-resistant spire-like flowers are always admired wherever they are planted. Why, then, are **Pentstemon Giant Hybrids** *(60 cm) not seen in our gardens more often? It cannot be that they are tender; they stand the winter in mild areas. Nor that they flower late; thousands of gardeners are happy to wait until August to see Asters in flower and they do not last as long as Pentstemons. Or that they have only one use; their cane-like stems, with long tapering spikes of trumpet-shaped flowers of crimson, scarlet, pink, rose and white are also superb for cutting.*

To me it remains a mystery: so do not overlook them if you want something for your garden that is not only beautiful but unusual as well.

Petunia

Modern plant breeders have worked on Petunias so successfully and for so many years that they are probably the most highly developed group of bedding plants in the world today. In hot dry climates and during warm sunny periods in cooler ones F1 hybrid Petunias leave every other bedding plant standing for their sheer overwhelming production of colour, submerging themselves beneath a canopy of flowers. Two basic types are available; grandifloras, with very large attractively waved or fringed flowers and multifloras, whose simpler flowers do not reach such impressive dimensions but instead are produced in astonishing profusion. Multifloras score again with much superior weather-resistance and recovery after rain, particularly in exposed situations, an important consideration with our climate. Choose multifloras for performance but in more sheltered situations plant grandifloras for their brazen flamboyance.

N.B. Don't bother with ordinary, non-hybrid varieties of either type – you wouldn't have backed Steptoe's nag against Red Rum would you?

Double forms of both types are available with flowers that resemble Carnations. Multiflora doubles may be massed in a really sunny and sheltered bed, but double grandifloras are best confined to windowboxes, tubs or similar containers. Neither do well in cold, open situations.

WHICH ONES TO GROW?

The number of F1 hybrid varieties is legion but you can plant with confidence any offered by your seedsman or retail nursery.

For special purposes choose the following:

Weather resistance Multiflora single varieties generally, but especially the **'Resisto' Series** (in blue, red, rose, salmon and white); **'Plum' Series** (blue, candy-pink, purple, sugar); **'Gypsy'** (coral-salmon) and **'Brass Band'** (primrose, the only yellow Petunia worth growing). Also, surprisingly, Grandiflora **'Pink Paradise'** (glowing rose-pink).

Windowboxes and Hanging Baskets All types are happy in containers but Grandiflora **'Cascade' Mixed** has been specially bred for these situations, as too has **'Jamboree' Mixed**, an extra large-flowered multiflora type.

Tubs, Patio Planters, and Strawberry Barrels Grandiflora single **'Cloud' Series** and **'Titan' Mixed** are extra large flowered, and particularly well suited to close-up viewing in these containers.

Petunia *'Gay Paris'.*

Petunia *'Astro'.*

Petunia *Grandiflora Mixture.*

Petunia *'Pink Cloud'.*

Phlox drummondii*

A fine and deservedly popular low-growing bedder, good for a hot sunny spot. Produces masses of brightly coloured flowers in clustered heads until severe frosts.

'Beauty' Mixed Early-flowering, bushy compact plants that withstand poor weather conditions well. 15 cm.

Rudbeckia*

Another superb late-summer-flowering plant that deserves much wider use. Will flower from mid-August through September while shrugging aside everything our climate likes to throw at it. Good for cutting too.

'Marmalade' Richest glowing yellow petals are perfectly contrasted by the dark central cone. Very free-flowering, a classic variety. 50 cm.
'Rustic Dwarfs' Counterpart to 'Marmalade', in shades of bronze, gold and mahogany. Same strong-stemmed, bushy, upright habit and equally reliable. 50 cm.

Salpiglossis*

An extravagantly exotic looking flower that you would expect to require the protection of a conservatory. However, it is very hardy and only needs a position that is sheltered from blustery winds. Probably better if direct sown where it is to flower. Velvety-textured trumpet flowers in gold, scarlet, rose, crimson, blue and mahogany are heavily veined and splashed with contrasting colours. ***'Splash'*** *is an F1 hybrid mixture that has improved vigour and earliness. Also makes good, if tall, pot plant. 50–60 cm.*

Salvia

Whether you love or loathe the intense scarlet colour of Salvia splendens, *you have to acknowledge that its remarkable ability to continue flowering in all conditions through the summer from June until autumn frost gives it a distinction that few other plants enjoy – certainly no other red ones.*

Phlox drummondii *Mixed.*

Rudbeckia *'Marmalade'.*

Salvia *'Blaze of Fire'.*

Salvia *'Dress Parade'.*

New varieties continue to appear and are worth trying but the old well-tried ones are still dependable – **'Blaze of Fire'** (30 cm), **'Scarlet Pygmy'** (15 cm) and **'Royal Mountie'** (30 cm). Newer introductions with handsome glossy dark-green foliage for contrast are **'Carabiniere'** (38 cm), **'Hot Shot'** (30 cm), **'Ryco'** (30 cm) and **'Vanguard'** (30 cm).

'Dress Parade' and **'Spectacular'** are two novelty mixtures that include rose, pink, purple, salmon and white in addition to scarlet and could extend the appeal of this fine plant. I feel that these other colours may not withstand the hottest sunshine as well as the scarlets but should do well in cooler situations or light, filtered shade. 35 cm.

Salvia farinacea

Entirely different from Salvia splendens *but an equally undemanding plant, weather-resistant, long-flowering and even hardier. Bushy upright plants have long-stemmed flower spikes that look just like Lavender.*

'Victoria' A really elegant soft violet-blue flower that will enhance any garden, one of the finest bedding plants you can grow. Flowers all through the summer. 45 cm.

Stocks*

The most commonly planted fragrant Bedding Plant, doing well in cool seasons. They prefer a rich, moist but well-drained soil. Drought they resent, particularly in the early stages when it can cause premature flowering from which the plants never recover. Another cause of failure is setting out plants that have become starved and hard; never be afraid to throw away such plants and start again with fresh young seedlings.

I prefer the normal **'Large Flowered Ten Week'** strain, which contains both double and single flowering plants for general use. (The **100% Double** types are less vigorous and their colours tend to be less intense, and on balance I don't feel they are worth the trouble.) 'Ten Week' Stocks make compact branched plants when well grown and the range of colours is very wide. The majority of flowers are fully double, in dense heavy spikes which last for a long time. 50 cm.

Sweet Peas – scented beauties.

Zinnia *'Scarlet Ruffles'.*

Sweet Peas*

The most extensively grown scented cut flower of any seed-raised Annual. Free-flowering tall traditional types of Sweet Peas are hardy and undemanding, requiring only reasonably fertile soil that can be kept well moistened, and support for their vigorous climbing vines. They can grow over 6 ft (180 cm) tall on trellis, wire or plastic netting, or when tied to canes or sticks. Requiring even less attention are new semi-dwarf varieties that form spreading mounds covered in flowers of equal quality and stem length to the tall types. These can be grown without supports, although short sticks or low netting gives a tidier appearance. All types may be sown in open ground April–May.

'Galaxy' Mixed Ever-blooming and exceptionally vigorous, this is the easiest of the tall types to grow. Extra long and strong stems, each carrying 5–7 large flowers are produced profusely over a very long period from early summer. 180 cm.
'Jet-Set' Mixed A fine, semi-dwarf strain, a magnificent sight when in full flower. Vigorous, short-jointed vines that are very easy to manage and with a little support from low netting or twigs will form a superb flowering hedge. Like 'Galaxy', 'Jet-Set' is a multiflora type in very bright and clear colours. 90 cm.

Plant breeders are concentrating on dwarf varieties. **'Little Elfin' Mixed** is a recent introduction, slightly dwarfer (75 cm) than 'Jet-Set', with a different range of colours; extra dwarf **'Patio' Mixed** can be used as an edging, in pots or even windowboxes.

Tagetes

Diminutive cousins to African and French Marigolds, and very dainty in comparison. Fine for edging, the mounded plants covering themselves quickly in single star-shaped flowers. ***'Golden Gem', 'Lemon Gem'*** *and* ***'Tangerine Gem'*** *are all dependable varieties. 20 cm.*

Verbena

A one-time favourite that is making a welcome return to our gardens. Good for massed bedding or edging and also first class for windowboxes and indoor pots. Many of the flowers are deliciously fragrant. All Verbenas are quite hardy and keep flowering through all conditions until the autumn.

New varieties are being produced but until these are tested and proven any of the following can be relied on:

'Olympia' Mixed Semi-erect plants that branch naturally and freely to produce neat bushes covered in clustered flowerheads in an unsurpassed range of colours. 30 cm.

'Sparkle' Mixed Low mounded spreading plants, quite different from 'Olympia'. Dense and free-flowering, most of the florets have an attractive white eye. 20 cm.

Zinnias*

We too rarely have summers in Britain that are warm and dry enough for these magnificent, brilliant flowers to show their paces. My advice must be to approach them with cautious optimism, balanced by determined stoicism in the face of possible failure! Moist warm soil is their prime requirement, with, at the same time, air that is warm but dry – a set of conditions that rarely occurs in these islands and almost impossible to create artificially.

New varieties are being introduced that, though expensive, offer hopes of success.

'Fruit Bowl' Mixed (F1 hybrid) Really massive fully double flowers like small teapots, on strong cane-like stems. The quilled and ruffled petals lend an informal quality to these brightly coloured monsters. 80–100 cm.

'Ruffles' Mixed (F1 hybrid) Good weather tolerance. Medium-sized flowers on straight stems are fine for cutting. The usual rainbow-like Zinnia colours. 60 cm.

'Peter Pan' Mixed (F1 hybrid) Dwarf bushy plants, vigorous and sturdy, stand up well to most conditions. Flowers are large, fully double and have quilled petals, produced when the plants are only 20 cm tall, making 'Peter Pan' a first-class subject for windowboxes, tubs and low massed beds or edging. Brilliant full colour range, but height and uniformity tend to vary between different colours. 30–40 cm.

Dramatic effects are easily achieved by careful planning.

Some Important Hardy Annuals

Probably the easiest of any type of flower you can grow and certainly the cheapest; nothing else gives you so much colour for such a small initial outlay. Nearly all have outstanding weather resistance and recovery. Sow seed from March onwards once the soil has become workable.

** These items can be sown in well-drained soil during late August/September if you have space available in your borders at that time.*

Alyssum*

The most widely grown dwarf white-flowered edging plant. Extremely adaptable, thrives in almost any situation without looking out of place and blooms throughout the summer. Will grow on rockeries, between paving stones, on walls and in windowboxes. In addition to white there are also pink, purple and lilac varieties which are generally less vigorous and need rather more careful placing for maximum effect.

'Snowcarpet', **'Snowcloth'**, and **'Snowdrift'** are fine, ground-hugging white forms that become mounds of pure white, sweet-scented flowers.
'Little Dorrit' has a more erect bush-like habit and **'Tiny Tim'** is extra dwarf.
Best of the coloured forms are rich purple **'Oriental Night'**, lilac-pink **'Rosie O'Day'** and deep pink **'Wonderland'**. 5–10 cm.

Bartonia

Will grow anywhere and flower all summer.

'Aurea' Large chalice-shaped flowers of glistening golden yellow. 45 cm.

Cabbage, Ornamental

These unusual and very decorative plants have been dubbed the Beau Brummels of the cabbage family! Bright rose-pink or cream centres are complimented by curled and fringed outer leaves with pink or cream veining. Colour improves with lower autumn temperatures. Highly decorative and in the last resort edible. Sow in May. 30 cm.

Calendula*

Nothing is easier to grow than these splendid 'English' or 'Pot' Marigolds with their distinctive aromatic foliage. Long a favourite for borders and cutting, new dwarf varieties make ideal bedding or windowbox subjects. Although sometimes disliked for the persistence of 'volunteer' seedlings, these are easily removed.

Of the many varieties to choose from, **'Pacific Beauty' Art Shades** (50–60 cm) has uncommon colouring combinations, from deepest flame-orange through yellow to cream. The stems are long for cutting. **'Fiesta Gitana'** (30 cm) is a new early-flowering, dwarf compact mixture which brings the easy simple culture of Calendula into the province of windowbox and container gardening. **'Family Circle'** is the latest British-bred introduction in this dwarf class.

Candytuft*

Quick-growing, fast-flowering plants for virtually any soil or situation except shade.

Needs to be sown in bold groupings for best effect. Available in red, rose and white separate colours and mixture.

'Fairy' Mixture (15 cm) Very dwarf and compact plants of exceptional uniformity, for mixed edging. Colours ranging from carmine, rose, pink and lavender to white.

Chrysanthemum tricolour

Very useful flowers for borders and cutting, available in either double or single forms. The single types have the greatest visual impact and are to be preferred for most situations. Most of the flowers have attractive central zones of a contrasting colour. Seed of white or yellow separate colours is available but mixtures are most usual.

'Court Jesters' Mixed At 45 cm this variety is only three-quarters the height of other mixtures, making it the first choice for bedding in our present-day small gardens. Strong bushy plants carry boldly zoned flowers in a very wide and bright colour range.
'Double' Mixed (60 cm) This mixture has a wide range of attractive colours. Some plants will carry single flowers.

Clarkia*

An indispensable flower for borders, among shrubs or any situation where its 60 cm height can be accommodated. The long sprays of exquisite double rosette flowers are excellent for cutting. This fine old cottage-garden flower used to be offered in a wide range of separate colours but only mixtures are now offered. Colours included are red, salmon, pink, mauve, carmine, purple and white.

Cornflower*

Another classic old English garden flower. Very hardy, fine for borders and cutting, there is also a dwarf variety that withstands rough weather well in more formal beds.

The typical **'Blue Ball'** type (90 cm) is also offered in a mixture of colours from blue, pink, and dark red to white. **'Polka Dot' Mixed** is the dwarf form (38–45 cm).

Dimorphotheca

'Star of the Veldt' is a fine, sun-loving plant, fast-growing and quick to flower. It has masses of glistening daisy-like flowers in shades of apricot, salmon-orange, bright orange, gold and lemon-yellow, and white. (30 cm.)

Alyssum *'Snowdrift'.*

Godetia *Dwarf Mixture.*

Eschscholzia*

Californian Poppies have brightly coloured poppy-like flowers, produced freely in full sun, even on poor dry soils. A real old-time favourite, and deservedly so. Any of the mixtures available will give complete satisfaction, but ***'Ballerina'*** *is a shade dwarfer at 25 cm and has unusually fluted flowers like a dancer's 'tutu'.*

Godetia*

Surely one of the glories of the Hardy Annual border, Godetias have long shared equal prominence with Clarkias in 'cottage garden' displays. Unlike Clarkias, some separate colours of Godetia can still be obtained and I urge all who appreciate the impact value of really beautiful, silken colouring en masse to search the garden centre seed racks for:

'Kelvedon Glory' (38 cm), **'Salmon Princess'** (25 cm) and **'Sybil Sherwood'** (38 cm). You will not be disappointed. Among mixtures **'Azalea-flowered'** (38 cm) has waved and frilled, semi-double flowers in many beautiful hues, while **'Tall Double' Mixed** (60 cm) is invaluable for cutting, having a very long vase life.

Larkspur*

Another classic flower, the 'Annual Delphinium' is tall and stately, the 'pikeman' of the Hardy Annual border. The double flowers, close-packed in long tapering spikes, are reminiscent of Stocks (without the scent, of course). Sow early in spring (March) since high day temperatures may inhibit germination; but for finest results of all sow in September.

'Giant Imperial' Mixed (90 cm) The finest variety, vigorous, erect base-branching habit giving many long stems. White, pink, red, blue, mauve and white, with intermediate shades. There is also a dwarf non-branching type (30 cm).

Lavatera

'Mallow' is always a beautiful flower but at 90–120 cm was just too tall and vigorous a plant to be as widely used as its floral qualities deserved. Lavatera has now been tamed by modern plant breeding; dwarfer, self-branching bush types have been introduced that enable these superb, free-flowering mallows to find a place in any garden. Sturdy, robust, and self-supporting if not overcrowded, there should be a place for at least one plant in every garden – they will make a specimen 'conversation piece'; a source of long-lasting cut-flowers; or plant them 60 cm apart and you have a unique flowering low hedge for the summer months. Probably the cheapest space fillers available.

'Silver Cup' (rose-pink) and **'Mont Blanc'** (snowy white) are the two new bush-growing varieties. It is important to allow them plenty of space – they can spread as much as 75–90 cm under good conditions – otherwise their vigour will force them to grow taller than their normal 60 cm.

Linaria*

Like dainty, miniature Snapdragons, 'Toad Flax' is quick to flower and continues over a long period. Dwarf and compact, suitable for edging as well as massed bedding.

'Fairy Bouquet' Mixed (20 cm) is the most compact variety, colours are very bright and varied, and it is recommended for any front-of-border situation.

Larkspurs are fine cut flowers.

Nasturtiums prefer sunny situations.

Mignonette

Another fragrant flower, and perhaps the most widely sown in English gardens. Mignonette has a very distinctive sweet scent which is produced during the day, thus making it a perfect companion to Matthiola bicornis. *Like Limnanthes, Mignonette is also much visited by bees. Prefers to be sown in a well-firmed seed bed. 25–30 cm.*

Nasturtium

Only Nasturtiums produce such brilliant sheets of colour in unpromising situations. Indeed, the one certain road to failure with it is to grow it in rich, fertile soil with lots of moisture – the result is a lot of plant but few, and invisible, flowers.

Although generally regarded as sun-lovers and haters of shade, Nasturtiums will perform miracles even below the shade-canopy of trees, provided that the soil conditions are really dry. (You will have to apply some water from time to time of course.) Dwarf (25 cm) and semi-dwarf (40 cm) types can be grown in most situations, while the tall climbing variety will ramble through a low bush or hedge, and brighten any trellis, back of border, or rough dry bank where nothing else will flourish. All types come in brilliant orange and yellow shades, scarlets and crimson.

The latest introductions are dwarf forms with spurless, upward facing flowers carried well above the leaves and forming a dense carpet of bloom. Fine, too, for hanging baskets, pots and containers where root-run is limited. **'Red Roulette'** is a blazing fiery orange-red, and **'Whirlybird'** is a mixture in the same style, embracing all the colours found in Nasturtiums. 25 cm.

Nigella*

'Love-in-a-Mist' is another old traditional favourite which we have all probably grown and marvelled at when allowed our first garden when very young. The feathery foliage, cornflower-like blossoms and curiously shaped seed pods all combine into an unforgettable childhood memory. However, Nigella is valued by adults, too, particularly flower arrangers for its unique qualities whether fresh cut or dried.

In addition to the typical blue **'Miss Jekyll'**, a range of colours is available in **'Persian Jewels' Mixed.** Both varieties are 45 cm.

Double Shirley Poppies.

Virginian Stocks.

Poppy*

Few flowers are as easy or undemanding in culture as the silken-petalled beauty **'Shirley Poppy'**. *From the scarlet sentinels of our cornfields – before the coming of chemical 'hoeing' – have been selected and bred an almost unbelievable range of colours and flower forms. Singles, doubles, brilliant self-colours, pastel shades and bicolours, their apparent fragility belies their robust vigour. At 70–75 cm they can't be crowded into any old corner, but do try to find a spot, however small, in a sunny situation where a sprinkle of seed can work its magic for you.*

Sunflower

With such robust vigour one is tempted to class Sunflowers as young trees or shrubs! However, Annuals they are, and very good ones too, well able to look after themselves and asking little more than to be planted and given space to grow. Everyone knows the 'Giant Single', with its huge head of seeds – a pie-feast for parrots – atop of its flagpole stem, up to 10 ft, but there are also varieties of more modest ambitions that fit more easily into a garden scheme, and well worth the space they occupy.

'Sunburst' has a neat branching habit, stems are wiry and colours of its single flowers range from pale primrose to bronze and maroon. Ideal cut flower and a modest 120 cm *(4 ft)*. **'Autumn Beauty'** is taller at 180 cm (6 ft).

Sweet Sultan

A relative of the Cornflower, the large fragrant flowers are in shades of pink, purple, mauve, yellow and white. Excellent for cutting and will flower all summer. 60 cm.

Virginian stock*

One of the best known and hardiest of all Annuals, Virginian Stock will grow almost anywhere. Its masses of red, lilac and white flowers look particularly well when grown in crevices in paving. A good plant to scatter in those odd corners. 20 cm.